THE VOCES8 METHOD

PAUL SMITH

PETERS EDITION LTD

A member of the EDITION PETERS GROUP

FRANKFURT/M. · LEIPZIG · LONDON · NEW YORK

Additional resources

THE VOCES8 APP

Encourage your students to make the VOCES8 Method their own. Build your own performances using the fully interactive app. Available from www.greshamcentre.com.

TRAINING SESSIONS

Led by members of VOCES8 and workshop training leaders from Voces Cantabiles Music, either at our education centre in central London or at your school. Contact paul@voces8.com for further information.

Peters Edition Limited
2–6 Baches Street
London
N1 6DN

Tel: 020 7553 4000
sales@editionpeters.com
www.editionpeters.com

First published 2013
© 2013 by Paul Smith

A catalogue record for this book is available from the British Library

Cover and inside design by Aptronym

Printed in England by Halstan & Co, Amersham, Bucks.

Paul Smith

Paul is the founder of Voces Cantabiles Music (VCM), a charity that works with more than 20,000 young people every year. He sings with VOCES8 and is the CEO of the charity. He is a passionate educationalist and musician.

With VOCES8, Paul performs each year in the UK, USA, Europe, Asia and Africa. Performance highlights include the Wigmore Hall and the Festival Hall in London; the National Centre of Performing Arts in Beijing, and Opera City in Tokyo. With VOCES8, Paul has recorded eight albums, winning three international a cappella awards in the process. VCM is based at the Gresham Centre, a centre for vocal excellence, education, inspiration and outreach at St Anne and St Agnes Church in the heart of the City of London.

Paul designs and leads workshop programmes for young people, teachers and business leaders across the UK and internationally. As a writer and arranger, Paul has composed and arranged music for choirs, children and for VOCES8 which has been performed at the Royal Opera House, Covent Garden; Alexandra Palace and around the world. He created the '21st-century Messiah' using Handel's music for a performance at the Foundling Museum.

Paul has written two children's musicals for students in Tower Hamlets, London: 'Around the World in 60 Minutes' and 'Street Cries of London', which were performed at Wilton's Music Hall with VOCES8 and students from local schools. He has also worked with the Children's Society on a project examining asylum conditions for young people in the UK.

Paul leads programmes for young leaders in the UK, France and the USA, and carries out public speaking and coaching engagements for sixth-form students and teachers on subjects such as 'The impact of creativity in modern society' and ''The VOCES8 Method'. 'The VOCES8 Method' is Paul's first book and he is delighted to be an ambassador for Edition Peters.

Acknowledgements

The VOCES8 Method has been many years in the making and, to that end, I could probably thank every teacher that has taught and trained me, all the students who have worked with me since 2006 and all of the musicians who have inspired me. There are, however, some very special people who have given their time and thoughts for nothing more than a shared passion and desire to make something useful which has a basis in music and education.

I'd like to acknowledge, first, Susan Hallam. It was her fine paper, 'The Power of Music' that really forced me to sit down and write this practical response to her findings. The full reference for the paper can be found at the back of the book for those who want to read it, and I can highly recommend it. Sue has been very supportive throughout. I'd like to extend my thanks to Sylwia Holmes and the Institute of Education more widely as well for their work on the pilot programme.

In coming up with the specific content of the layers, I was very grateful to have some fine teachers and musicians to test my theories on. John Padley, Ann Wright, Simon Lock, Xanthe Sarr and Peter Davies have all taken time to study the book and make suggestions for ways in which it could be tweaked. They have also been key members of the team that has helped me stage the pilot scheme in Hackney, Slough, Rutland and Berkshire.

I'm lucky enough to spend all of my time surrounded by world-class musicians, and I need to thank all of the members of VOCES8, Apollo5, and the VCM team for their efforts and support in this endeavour, and for their inspiration in everything else that they do. This book is, in part, designed to bottle the work that these excellent music leaders deliver in schools around the world on a daily basis. Special thanks to Clare Stewart, who has been on hand to offer positive critical analysis and fantastic design ideas from the moment I started out on this adventure.

The design of this book has been debated at great length. For his wisdom and creativity, I need to say a hearty thanks to Matthew Banwell from Aptronym. It is because of him that this book is so beautifully and cleanly laid out. Coming up with a design that made it possible to interpret musical ideas written in a non-musical format has taken a great deal of thought. I would also like to thank Peter Dart, a friend and supporter of VOCES8, who kindly gave me his input with regard to the overall concept of the VOCES8 Method. He has considerable expertise, and his assistance was highly valuable to me.

The team at Edition Peters has been supportive in every way imaginable. Equally passionate about music and music education, committed to creating something unique and questioning me along every step of the way, they have experience and knowledge in spades, and I could not have published this book without their input. A particular thanks to Linda Hawken, Andrew Hanley and Robin Tyson.

Finally, to my friends and family. To my parents who foolishly agreed to be guinea pigs for the first four stages at a family BBQ, and to everyone who has sat around clicking and clapping just to please me. Music is made in groups, with friends and when people get together in formal and informal settings. It's about expressing emotion, fun, and sharing something special. Music was here before us and will be here afterwards. Thanks to my friends and family, who get to live through our version of it.

Paul Smith

Contents

Introduction

A new start to the school day

Based on a research paper from the Institute of Education, The VOCES8 Method exists to have a positive impact on how students learn.

The Method will better prepare students for their school day and develop key learning skills which will have a conscious and sub-conscious effect on their academic learning process.

The primary aim of The VOCES8 Method is the search for improved academic results for pupils across the whole school in the spheres of numeracy, literacy and linguistics.

There are additional benefits to be gained in the areas of physical and mental health; self-awareness; confidence; teamwork; problem solving; and creative thinking.

This method has been developed with the aid of a research paper by Susan Hallam from the Institute of Education in London and seven years of practical testing by Paul Smith in a variety of academic settings globally. The pilot programme for this specific project is happening in the UK and the USA in 2012–13.

The VOCES8 Method draws on research into specific aspects of music-making that demonstrate quantifiable transfer into improved academic results.

This Method provides a simple tool that has universal application and limitless opportunities for growth.

The 8 Voices Method... The VOCES8 Method. Designed by Paul Smith, founder of VOCES8.

This course provides a simple learning tool with eight stages of development for schools to work through.

To run this course, you could use:

8 minutes for a full school assembly (or class) each week
1 trained leader
7 assistants (maximum)
8 microphones
1 PA
An open mind

Instructions

- Set the stage while the hall is empty with one chair and one microphone on a stand.

- When ready to start, walk onto the stage and sit down with the microphone.

- Welcome everyone in a way that requires a response.

- Outline the following instructions:

1. If I do this (move your finger in a circular motion), that means keep going.

2. If I do this (move your hand from low to high) that means get louder.

3. If I do this (move your hand from high to low), that means get quieter.

4. If I do this (clench your fist) that means stop.

- These are the only physical instructions you will need to give.

- Make sure that any instruction you give is clear, visible, and as large as you can make it.

- Say 'copy me'. Pause. Begin.

Use this code to watch a video demonstration of these instructions

1 Introduction and leading into pop rhythm

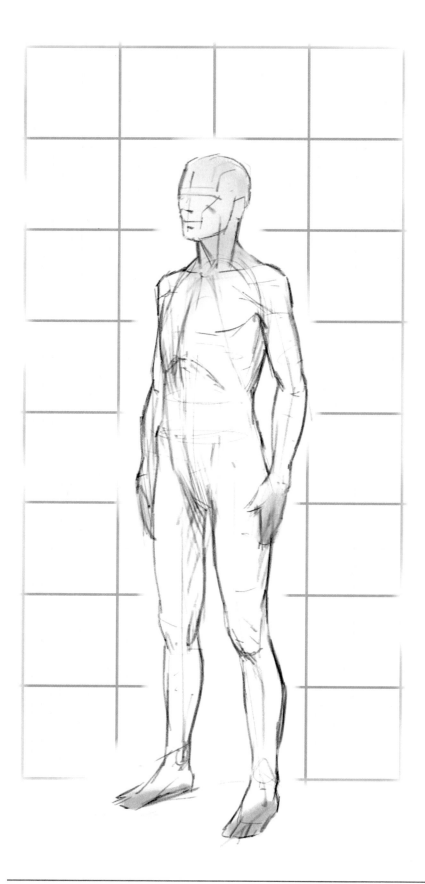

BODY POSITION

YOU: 1, 2, 3, 4 (counting the numbers on one hand).

THEM: They copy you.

YOU: Repeat twice (counting the numbers on one hand the first time and on two hands the second time).

THEM: They copy you.

YOU: 1, 2, 3, 4, 5

Do this three times (counting numbers on one hand, then two).

THEM: They copy you.

YOU: 1, 2... 4, 5

Do this three times missing out different numbers each time (and doing the same with one and then two hands).

THEM: They copy you.

Introducing physical actions (movements happen with a rhythmic beat):

YOU (still speaking numbers):

1	2	3	4
Left arm out	Left arm up	Left arm out	Left arm down

THEM: They copy you.

YOU:
1	2	3	4
Right arm out	Right arm up	Right arm out	Right arm down

THEM: They copy you.

YOU: Repeat two or three times. You can vary the tempo if you want to.

1	2	3	4
Left hand slap thigh	Right hand click	Single clap	Right hand click

THEM: They copy you.

YOU: Double the length of this pattern and repeat. Set a steady tempo now.

THEM: They copy you.

YOU: Dum. Tea. Quiche. Tea.

THEM: They copy you.

YOU: Now without the vowels: Dm. T. Ksh. T.

THEM: Dm. T. Ksh. T.

YOU: Let's put this together:

1 Left hand slap thigh	2 Right hand click	3 Single clap	4 Right hand click

THEM: They copy you.

YOU:

Dm Left hand slap thigh	2 Right hand click	3 Single clap	4 Right hand click

THEM: They copy you.

YOU:

Dm Left hand slap thigh	T Right hand click	3 Single clap	4 Right hand click

THEM: They copy you.

YOU:

Dm Left hand slap thigh	T Right hand click	Ksh Single clap	4 Right hand click

THEM: They copy you.

YOU:

Dm Left hand slap thigh	T Right hand click	Ksh Single clap	T Right hand click

THEM: They copy you.

YOU: Repeat this final stage twice.

THEM: They copy you.

YOU: Use instruction 1 ⏵.

THEM: They should continue this rhythmic pulse.

While they continue, say to them (in time with the pulse):

Keep	it	stea-	dy.	Don't	speed	up.	
1	2	3	4	1	2	3	4

THEM: They should continue this rhythmic pulse.

YOU: Use instruction 2 🔊 to raise the volume level of the group.

THEM: They should react to this instruction.

Note: If they don't react, do the action again whilst saying, in time with the pulse:

Get-	ting	Lou-	der
1	2	3	4

Do the action once more after this, and they should respond.

YOU: Use instruction 3 🙂.

THEM: They should react to this instruction.

Let them continue two more times quietly before using instruction 2 🔊 again.

Once the group is loud again, let them carry on twice more.

YOU: Give the group a count of four and then use instruction 4 ⏹ to stop them.

Use this code to watch a demonstration of the introduction and the pop beat.

E N D   O F   S T A G E   1

2 Pop beat & African rhythm

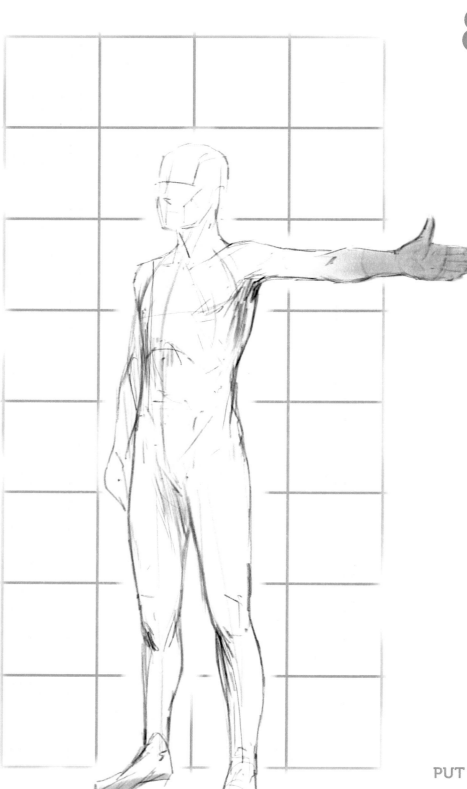

PUT YOUR LEFT ARM OUT

Start this session in the same way as session 1. As you continue this programme, the group you are leading will respond with ever increasing accuracy to the opening section. When the group is completely comfortable with Stage 1, they will naturally have improved their basic abilities of co-ordination and pulse. Once this has happened you can vary the opening part of the session as follows:

- Speed (tempo) – try getting the group used to faster and slower speeds with the pop tempo.

- Different body actions. Try:

1	2	3	4
Clap	Left hand click	Right hand click	Clap

This is quite easy. You can also try this, which is more of a challenge:

1	2	3	4
Clap	Left hand click	Right hand slap thigh	Right hand click

Introducing The Standard Pattern, one of the key rhythms to be heard on the Yaruba Bata Drum:

The final sequence will look like this:

1	2	3	4	5	6	7	8	9	10	11	12	13	14	15	16
x	–	–	x	–	–	x	x	–	–	x	–	x	–	–	x

In the sequence above, the 'x' marks a clap or, when this is vocalized, a 'cha'.

Now let's build this up:

YOU:

1	2	3	4
Clap	Left hand click	Right hand click	Clap

THEM: They copy you.

YOU: Repeat this once and then continue as follows:

1	2	3	4
Clap			Clap

THEM: They copy you.

YOU: Repeat this twice and then change to:

1	2	3	4
		Clap	Clap

THEM: They copy you.

YOU: Repeat this twice and then change to:

1	2	3	4
		Clap	

THEM: They copy you.

YOU: Repeat this twice and then change to:

1	2	3	4
Clap			Clap

THEM: They copy you.

YOU: Repeat this once and then add as follows:

Now introduce the spoken word while clapping the pulse of four:

1	2	3	4
Cha			Cha

THEM: They copy you.

YOU: Repeat this twice and then change to:

1	2	3	4
		Cha	Cha

THEM: They copy you.

YOU: Repeat this twice and then change to:

1	2	3	4
		Cha	

THEM: They copy you.

YOU: Repeat this twice and then change to:

1	2	3	4
Cha			Cha

YOU: Repeat this twice.

Now go back to clapping the rhythm and speaking the numbers. You're going to put together the rhythm now, with the first half to begin with:

1	2	3	4	5	6	7	8
Clap			Clap			Clap	Clap

THEM: They copy you.

YOU: Repeat this twice and then change to:

1	2	3	4	5	6	7	8
		Clap		Clap			Clap

YOU: Repeat this twice and then change this to speaking 'cha' and clapping the pulse:

1	2	3	4	5	6	7	8
Cha			Cha			Cha	Cha

THEM: They copy you.

YOU: Repeat this twice and then change to:

1	2	3	4	5	6	7	8
		Cha		Cha			Cha

YOU: Repeat this twice and then say 'Now it's time to put the whole thing together, which looks like this':

1	2	3	4	5	6	7	8	9	10	11	12	13	14	15	16
Clap			Clap			Clap	Clap		Clap		Clap				Clap

THEM: They copy you.

YOU: Repeat this twice and then drop out the numbers, replacing them with 'Cha' to go with each clap and 'd' in place of the numbers with no clap. It looks like this:

Cha	d	d	Cha	d	d	Cha	Cha	d	d	Cha	d	Cha	d	d	Cha
Clap			Clap			Clap	Clap			Clap		Clap			Clap

THEM: They copy you.

YOU: Give them instruction 1 ▶ so that they keep going.

While they keep this going, you now leave them and demonstrate layering the pop rhythm over the group as they continue with the standard pattern.

It should look like this:

THEM:

Cha	d	d	Cha	d	d	Cha	Cha	d	d	Cha	d	Cha	d	d	Cha
Clap			Clap			Clap	Clap			Clap		Clap			Clap

YOU:

1	2	3	4	5	6	7	8	9	10	11	12	13	14	15	16
Dm	t	ksh	t	Dm	t	ksh	t	Dm	t	ksh	t	Dm	t	ksh	t

After letting this run round three times, bring the whole group to a stop using instruction 4 ◎.

Now divide the group into two – split them straight down the middle if possible, so one group is on your right and the other on your left. Give them names.

First, start Group 1 off with the pop drum beat. Start them as follows:

YOU: Ready? After 4. (Now, counting to four with the pulse you want, and using your fingers to count for them as well):

1, 2, 3, 4... (and they should all come back in with you):

1	2	3	4
Left hand slap	Right hand click	Single clap	Right hand click
Dm	t	ksh	t

GROUP 1:

YOU: Use instruction 1 ▶ with this group so that they continue without you.

Now turn to Group 2:

YOU: Now, with the African rhythm... Ready? 1, 2, 3, 4 (counting on your fingers again to count them in):

GROUP 2:

Cha	d	d	Cha	d	d	Cha	Cha	d	d	Cha	d	Cha	d	d	Cha
Clap			Clap			Clap	Clap			Clap		Clap			Clap

YOU: Use instruction 1 ▶ with this group so that they continue without you.

Hint: You might find it helps the group doing the African rhythm to have you do it with them a couple of times before leaving them to it.

Once both rhythms are going, use instruction 3 ⊗ to make both groups quieter. Then use instruction 2 ⊗ to make both groups louder again. When the groups do this for the first time, they may find it hard to keep the steady pulse going. If this happens, you can lead either group as necessary to re-establish the pulse.

When both groups are as loud as they can get, signal that you are going to stop. Give them a count of four and then use instruction 4 ◉ to stop them. Try to do this as Group 2 reaches the end of it's longer rhythm.

Note An extra person: if you have someone who is confident enough to be your assistant, this would be a good time to get them involved. It's possible to do this session by yourself, but it would be great to have someone act as the leader for Group 1 while you lead Group 2. Getting someone involved at this early stage will be of real benefit in later sessions.

When you have an extra person: make sure that you introduce them to the group in a way which will make the assistant feel confident. You can get the group to cheer for your brave assistant, or give them a round of applause. Whatever you do, be clear before you start that the group is going to follow your assistant. Give clear directions to your assistant – as you would to the group you are leading.

A note on the African rhythm involved in this session:

Many sub-Saharan languages do not have a word for rhythm, or even for music. Rhythms represent the very fabric of life and embody the people's interdependence in human relationships. Cross-beats can symbolize challenging moments or emotional stress: playing them while fully grounded in the main beats prepares one for maintaining life-purpose while dealing with life's challenges.

The sounding of three beats against two is experienced in everyday life and helps develop "a two-dimensional attitude to rhythm". Throughout western and central Africa, child's play includes games that develop a feeling for multiple rhythms.

Use this code to watch Paul demonstrate the Standard Pattern rhythm.

E N D   O F   S T A G E   2

3 Pop beat, African rhythm and a first melodic line

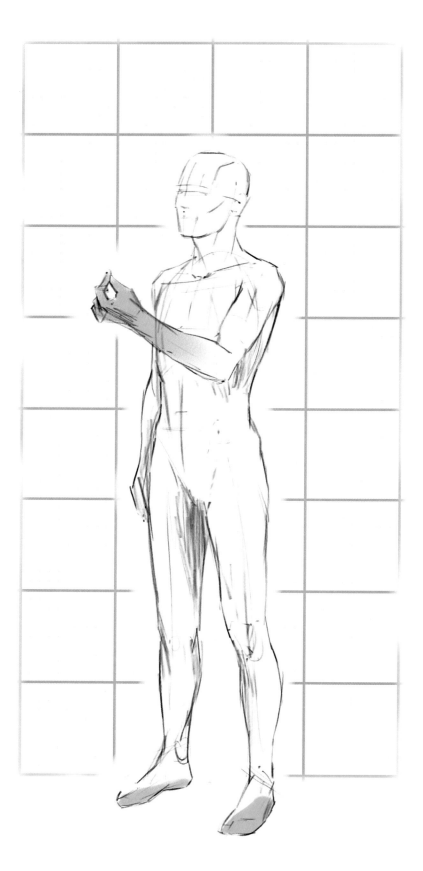

CLICK YOUR FINGERS

By the time you reach stage three, the group will have understood how the rest of the process is going to work, and you will have begun to develop the layering of patterns. It is this layering process which is going to create music that sounds increasingly complex.

I hope you finished Stage 2 with an assistant to help you, and I would now like you to have that assistant join you again and, if possible, for you to welcome a second assistant to the stage. Until they are needed to work independently, these two assistants should lead the whole group when responding to your instructions.

Make sure you always introduce assistants.

At the beginning of Stage 3, start with a little session, as in Stage 1 and Stage 2, of introduction work, and with some of the variations outlined in Stage 2.

After this, set up the pop beat (and see what happens if you start with the full pattern, rather than by building it up).

YOU: Ready? After 4.

(Now, counting to four with the pulse you want, and using your fingers to count for them as well):

1, 2, 3, 4... (and they should all come back in with you):

GROUP 1:

Dm	T	Ksh	T
Left hand slap thigh	Right hand click	Single clap	Right hand click

THEM: They copy you.

YOU: Repeat this a few times and then use instructions 2 🔆 and 3 🔅 to change the volume. When you are happy that everyone is following you, use instruction 4 ⊚ to stop the group.

Now you can introduce a variation to the pop beat.

You can see that an extra 'T' has been added in the fourth beat. Each '&' happens halfway between the numbers. So, the extra 'T' comes halfway between the '4' and the '1'.

YOU: Now listen to this:

1	&	2	&	3	&	4	&
Dm		T		Ksh		T	T

THEM: They copy you.

YOU: Repeat this a couple of times:

THEM: They copy you.

YOU: Repeat this a couple of times and then use instruction 4 ⊙ to stop them.

Now, still with the whole group, have a practice with the Standard rhythm from Stage 2.

Cha	d	d	Cha	d	d	Cha	Cha	d	d	Cha	d	Cha	d	d	Cha
Clap			Clap			Clap	Clap			Clap		Clap			Clap

Ready? After 4.

(Now, counting to four with the pulse you want, and using your fingers to count for them as well):

1, 2, 3, 4...' (and they should all come back in with you):

THEM: They copy you.

YOU: Use instruction 1 ⊙ so that they can carry on. Repeat this with them 2 or 3 times before using instruction 4 ⊙ to stop the group.

All of this work is building on the previous session, helping the group you are leading reach a point at which they are comfortable with the different rhythms you are working with.

Introducing a melody.

Until now, the pitch of any of the rhythmic work has not been something that has needed to be unified. At this point in stage three, it's time to introduce the first element of a melodic line.

If you're not happy reading music, that's no problem. We're going to work from a keyboard diagram.

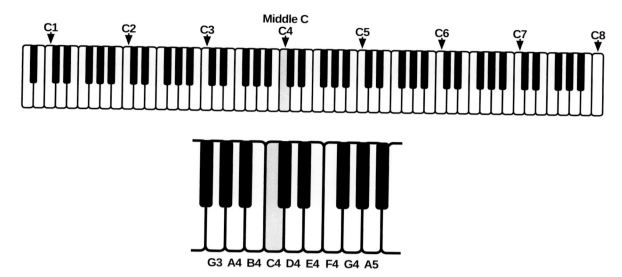

G3 A4 B4 C4 D4 E4 F4 G4 A5

On the diagram above you can see 'Middle C'. This is the first note you are going to sing to the students.

The first snippet of melody that you're going to sing in this session has four notes and starts with 'Middle C'. It then goes up one white note to D4, then down two to B4 and then comes back to C4 (Middle C).

You're going to use a different syllable for each note, and it's going to work with a pulse, like this:

YOU:	1	&	2	&	3	&	4	&
	Doh		Ray		Ti		Doh	
	C4		D4		B4		C4	

Repeat this twice, singing 'Doh-Ray-Ti-Doh' and counting the numbers on your fingers at the same time.

At this stage, to help everyone, the melody is on the beat.

YOU: Ok, everyone, repeat after me (still speaking only): 'Doh'

THEM: 'Doh'

YOU: 'Ray'

THEM: 'Ray'

YOU: 'Ti' (pronounced like 'Tea'!)

THEM: 'Ti'

YOU: 'Doh'

THEM: 'Doh'

YOU: Repeat this pattern speaking with different volumes.

Now add in the pop beat actions and do the whole pattern, like this:

1	2	3	4
Doh	Ray	Ti	Doh
Left hand slap	Right hand click	Single clap	Right hand click

THEM: They copy you.

YOU: Repeat this twice.

THEM: They copy you.

YOU: Now add in the notes whilst still doing the actions and using the syllables.

1	2	3	4
Doh	Ray	Ti	Doh
C4	D4	B4	C4
Left hand slap	Right hand click	Single clap	Right hand click

THEM: They copy you.

YOU: Repeat, and then use instruction 1 ▶ to tell them to continue this pattern. While they are doing this, use instructions 2 ⊛ and 3 ◉ to see how they respond.

Once you are happy that they are confident with this, use instruction 4 ◉ to stop them.

YOU: Fantastic. Well done. Now, let's try something slightly different:

(At this point, if you have one or two assistants to help you, it's time for them to demonstrate some layers with you). Assistant 1 should continue the pop beat. Assistant 2 should add the African rhythm layer on top of this.

You start by singing the Doh-Ray-Ti-Doh motif as it was being done previously, and then you change the rhythm to this:

1	&	2	&	3	&	4	&
Doh			Ray				
C4			D4				

5	&	6	&	7	&	8	&
Ti			Doh				
B4			C4				

This will give a syncopated feel to the rhythm. Note that both 'Ray' and the last 'Doh' come half way between the main beats.

This should fit with the other rhythms like this:

Cha	d	d	Cha	d	d	Cha	Cha	d	d	Cha	d	Cha	d	d	Cha
Clap			Clap			Clap	Clap			Clap		Clap			Clap

1	2	3	4	5	6	7	8	9	10	11	12	13	14	15	16
Dm	t	ksh	t	Dm	t	ksh	t	Dm	t	ksh	t	Dm	t	ksh	t

1	2	&	3	4	5	6	&	7	8	9	10	&	11	12	13	14	&	15	16
Doh	Ray				Ti			Doh		Doh	Ray				Ti			Doh	

Once you and your two assistants have demonstrated this three-layer series to the group, divide the main group into three sections (divide the room into thirds with splits from front to back, rather than sideways). Group 1 should be on your left, Group 2 should be in the middle and Group 3 should be on your right.

Now set up your two assistants and build up the music one layer at a time as follows:

Assistant 1 with Group 1; Assistant 2 with Group 2; you with Group 3.

YOU: Ok, Group 1 starts with the pop beat. Are you ready? Here we go. After four... 1, 2, 3, 4 (counting with your hand as in the previous Stage)...

ASSISTANT 1 WITH GROUP 1:

1	2	3	4	5	6	7	8	9	10	11	12	13	14	15	16
Dm	t	ksh	t	Dm	t	ksh	t	Dm	t	ksh	t	Dm	t	ksh	t

Use instruction 1 ⏵ to keep the group going. Also say to the group: 'Ok, Group 1, everyone keep watching and working with (name of Assistant 1)'.

Then, while Group 1 is still going, turn to Group 2 and say:

YOU: Ok, Group 2 starts with the African rhythm, and keep in time with Group 1. Are you ready? Here we go. After four... 1, 2, 3, 4...

ASSISTANT 2 WITH GROUP 2:

Cha	d	d	Cha	d	d	Cha	Cha	d	d	Cha	d	Cha	d	d	Cha
Clap			Clap			Clap	Clap			Clap		Clap			Clap

Use instruction 1 ▶ to keep the group going. Also say to the group: 'Ok, Group 2, everyone keep watching and working with (name of Assistant 2)'.

Then, while Group 1 and Group 2 are still going, turn to Group 3 and say:

YOU: Ok, this group starts with me on the melody, and keep in time with Group 1 and 2. Are you ready? Here we go. After four... 1, 2, 3, 4...

YOU WITH GROUP 3:

1	2	&	3	4	5	6	&	7	8	9	10	&	11	12	13	14	&	15	16
Doh		Ray				Ti		Doh			Doh		Ray			Ti		Doh	

Use instruction 1 ▶ to keep this group going.

Now step into the middle, while ensuring that Group 3 (your group) is going to stay in time and on pitch without you and lead all the groups in dynamic changes (using instructions 2 ⊕ and 3 ⊖).

Once you have done this, signal to Group 1 to watch you.

YOU: Group 1, watching me...1, 2, 3, 4 Stop!' (Use instruction 4 ⊙ to stop Group 1).

Let Group 1 listen for a couple of times through the pattern and then say:

YOU: Group 1, joining back in again, after 4... Ready... 1, 2, 3, 4 Go!

Group 1 joins back in again.

Do the same with Group 2.

Once all three groups are back in, bring the volume up as loud as you can.

YOU: Ok, everyone, watching me... after 4... 1, 2, 3, 4 STOP! (Using as big a version of instruction 4 ⊙ as you can).

Well done everyone, great work.

DO:

RAY:

MI:

FA:

SOL:

LA:

TI:

DO:

THE SOLFEGE SYLLABLES

Notes: This stage, and all of the future stages, will talk about using assistants to help you build the layers of music. It is possible to lead these stages without any assistants. You will need to set up each group and just allow a little more time for them to find a good rhythm and feel confident with what they are doing before you move on to set up the next layer of the music.

If, at any point, the groups get out of time with each other, simply stop them and then restart with a good count of 4 and by encouraging them to 'Keep It Steady' – just like in Stage 1.

Kodály: The Kodály Method, also referred to as the Kodály Concept, is an approach to music education developed in Hungary during the mid-twentieth century by Zoltán Kodály. His philosophies regarding education were further developed over a number of years by his associates and served as an inspiration for this method.

The melody in this section incorporates solfege syllables. You can also incorporate movement into the vocal section of Stage 3 by using the appropriate hand signal for the syllables you are singing. See the diagram (left) for an explanation on what to use, and make your signals strong and clear.

Use this code to watch Paul demonstrate the first melody and a variation.

END OF STAGE 3

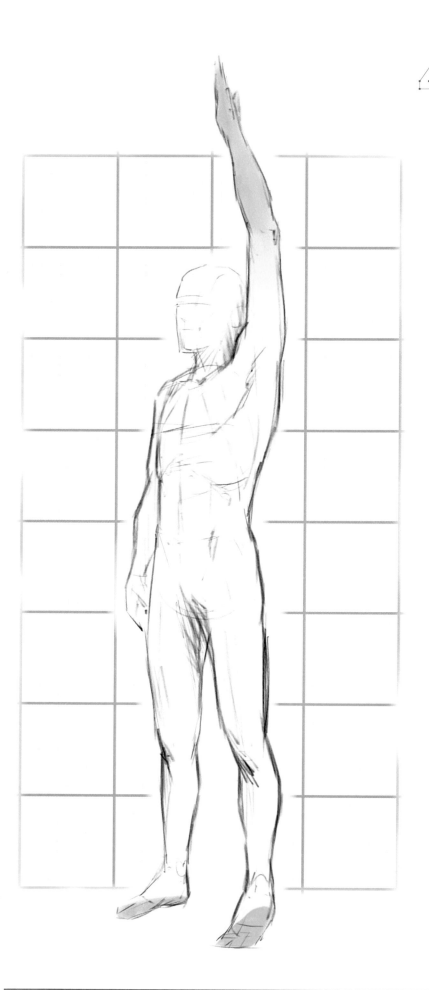

4 Pop beat melody 1 & Latin-American rhythm

PUT YOUR LEFT ARM UP

As we move into Stage 4, both you and the group you're leading are really beginning to get the hang of things. In this section, it's time to learn a Latin-American based rhythm.

You are now familiar with the way you start each session with some variants on the exercises in Stage 1, the method of demonstration and participation and the technique of building up the different parts step by step. You are also now familiar with the simple set of rules that you use to control the involvement and volume of each group.

As with the earlier stages, this section will get the group moving physically to the rhythm, which is such an important element of the brain training that we want to be working on in the VOCES8 Method.

In this section you still only need two assistants, but it would be a great idea, if you have the choice, to bring a third assistant up onto the stage to lead with you.

In the previous stage, we developed the pop beat by adding one extra 'T'. Now let's add another one:

YOU: Ok, let's start where we left off... Copy me:

1	&	2	&	3	&	4	&
Dm		T		Ksh		T	T

THEM: They copy you.

YOU: Repeat this twice (not forgetting the physical movement to accompany the rhythm) and then add in an extra 'T' like this:

1	&	2	&	3	&	4	&
Dm		T	T	Ksh		T	T

THEM: They copy you.

YOU: Repeat this a couple of times and then stop them using instruction 4 ◎.

After this, move on to Melody 1. We're going to learn a new variation of this too.

Remember that this melodic snippet starts on 'Middle C', or C4 on this diagram:

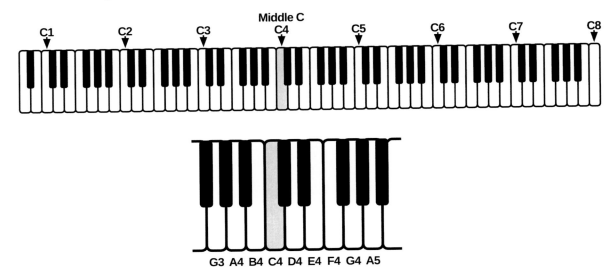

G3 A4 B4 C4 D4 E4 F4 G4 A5

And that the melody looks like this:

1	&	2	&	3	&	4	&
Doh				Ray			
C4				D4			

5	&	6	&	7	&	8	&
Ti				Doh			
B4				C4			

YOU: (Using the hand actions from the Stage 3 notes): OK, copy me:

1	&	2	&	3	&	4	&
Doh				Ray			
C4				D4			

5	&	6	&	7	&	8	&
Ti				Doh			
B4				C4			

THEM: They copy you. Repeat this a couple of times and then stop them using instruction 4 ◉.

YOU: Great, now we're going to change the melody just a little bit. Listen to this:

1	&	2	&	3	&	4	&
Doh			Ray		Me	Ray	
C4			D4		E4	D4	

5	&	6	&	7	&	8	&
Ti			Doh				
B4			C4				

You'll notice that we have added 'Me-Ray' into the first half of this melody. This brings in a new note (E4), which is just one step (or one white note on the keyboard) above D4.

THEM: They copy you. Repeat this twice and then stop the group using instruction 4 ◎.

YOU: Great stuff. Ok... now copy this (you speak this):

1	a	&	a	2	a	&	a

THEM: They copy you. Repeat this twice.

Then add in a clap like this:

YOU:

1	a	&	a	2	a	&	a
Clap			Clap	Clap		Clap	

THEM: They copy you. Repeat this twice.

YOU: And now like this:

1	a	&	a	2	a	&	a
Clap			Clap			Clap	

THEM: They copy you. Repeat this a few times until everyone is confident with it, and then use instruction 4 ◎ to stop the group.

YOU: Excellent. Now let's swap it around:

1	2	3	4	5	6	7	8
Clap	Clap	Clap	Clap	Clap	Clap	Clap	Clap
Cha			Cha			Cha	

THEM: They copy you. Repeat this again until everyone is confident with it, and then use instruction 4 ◎ to stop the group.

YOU: Ok, now let's take this one step further:

1	2	3	4	5	6	7	8
Clap			Clap			Clap	
Cha			Cha			Cha	

THEM: They copy you.

Repeat this a few times and then stop the group with... you guessed it, instruction 4 ◉. Note here that the group is having to feel the space between the numbers. This is a very important part of the process and will be difficult to begin with: it can take some time for a group to 'feel the silence' together.

Now the students have learned the 'Tresillo' (pronounced in English 'treh-see-yo'). We'll develop this into a 'Clave' in the next section, and this is also the basis for the 'Habanera'. This rhythm, as you will see, also links strongly with the previous African rhythm learned in stage 2.

Now, using your three assistants, it's time to put these layers together. Using the same format as in stage 3, starting one group at a time. Start with the pop beat:

YOU: Ok, let's start. After me... ready... 1, 2, 3, 4:

1	&	2	&	3	&	4	&
Dm		T	T	Ksh		T	T

ASSISTANT 1 AND GROUP 1:

They copy you. Repeat this twice and then signal to keep them going with instruction 1 ◉.

Note: When you're putting the layers together here, make sure that you're counting the numbers 1, 2, 3, 4, etc. at the same speed, regardless of how much is fitting into each beat. When you're practicing before you lead this session, do play around with doing all of these different rhythms at varying speeds. The more you practice, the more natural all of this will feel.

Now set up the next layer:

YOU: Ok, copy me and then continue:

1	&	2	&	3	&	4	&
Doh				Ray		Me	Ray
C4				D4		E4	D4

5	&	6	&	7	&	8	&
Ti				Doh			
B4				C4			

ASSISTANT 2 AND GROUP 2:

They copy you and then you use instruction 1 ▶ to keep this group going as well.

Now add in the next layer:

YOU: Ok, Group 3... Ready...? Here we go:

1	2	3	4	5	6	7	8
Clap			Clap			Clap	
Cha			Cha			Cha	

ASSISTANT 3 AND GROUP 3:

They copy you and then you use instruction 1 ▶ to keep this group going with the other two.

Once all three groups are up and running, use instructions 2 🅐 and 3 🅥 to change the volume of the whole group, and then the groups individually. This will allow each group to hear what the other groups are doing, and will help them get a feel for the piece of music that they are creating.

As in Stage 3, you can now try dropping out different groups and bringing them back in again. Still, just by using the four basic instructions, you are able to create, with the group, a dynamic and flowing piece of music.

Once this is working, you might like to try swapping the groups around, so they each get to have a go at the different layer that can be added in.

When the pattern is well established and you've played around with these ideas...

YOU: Ok, everybody watching me... ready...? 1, 2, 3, 4 STOP! (use instruction 4 ⏹ to bring them all off together).

DID YOU KNOW?

In setting up the pop beat alongside the tresillo, you're achieving a rhythmic base called Dem Bow.

The Dem Bow Riddim itself was first produced by Jamaican dancehall DJs in the late 1980s. At the heart of Dem Bow lies the 3+3+2 or tresillo rhythm, complemented by bass drums in 4/4 time.

To get the accurate feel for this, you need to double the speed of the tresillo rhythm in Stage 4 so that it fits with the Pop Beat Rhythm like this:

1	a	&	a	2	a	&	a
Dm				T		T	
Clap			Clap			Clap	

3	a	&	a	4	a	&	a
Ksh				T		T	
Clap			Clap			Clap	

'Riddim' is the Jamaican Patois pronunciation of the English word "rhythm," but in dancehall/reggae it refers to the instrumental accompaniment of a song.

END OF STAGE 4

5 Latin-American rhythm with Asian pentatonic scale and vocal inflections

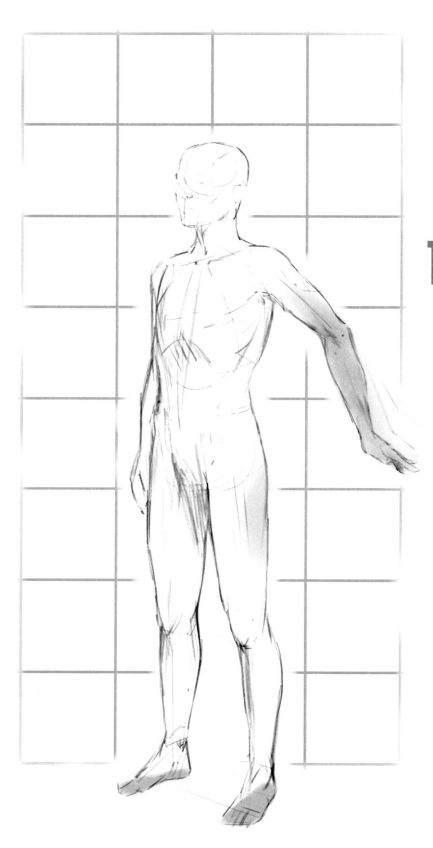

SLAP YOUR THIGH

As we move into Stage 5, you're getting a really good feel for how the layering game works.

Below is a graph that shows how a five-way layering game can work. This is a simple version in four sections, but once you get the idea, the number of sections and options you can play with are endless.

Music is all about the creation of layers and the way in which each layer works with the other layers. It can be amazing to be a part of a group which is putting these layers together. As you move through Stage 5, we're bringing in another new element – this time using a musical scale common in Japan (and elsewhere) – and you'll also learn how to extend a couple of the ideas from the previous sections.

Now... have a look at this little graph:

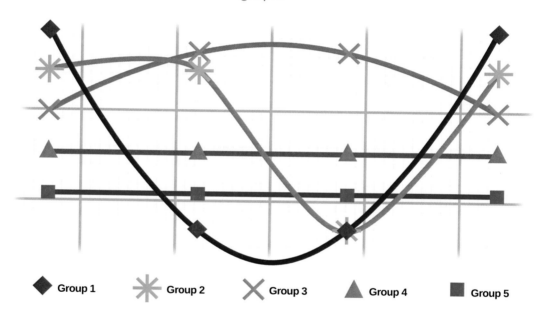

♦ **Group 1**   ✳ **Group 2**   ✕ **Group 3**   ▲ **Group 4**   ■ **Group 5**

In this graph, you can imagine that each line is one of the musical layers that you have been teaching to your group.

Now, let's look at what each line does in this graph:

GROUP 1: Group one starts loud, gets quieter, stops during the second section, starts quietly and then builds again in volume.

GROUP 2: Dips down to nothing very quickly at the start of section 3 and then builds again..

GROUP 3: Gets louder during the second section and then comes back down to the original volume.

GROUP 4: Provides a solid line throughout.

GROUP 5: As with group 4.

Now, why not try to imagine this on a bigger scale? Good luck, and have fun.

The Clave Rhythm

Now, it's time to develop the Tresillo rhythm a little (I did promise, didn't I?). We're going to turn this into a 'Clave' rhythm, and it looks like this:

1	a	&	a	2	a	&	a
Clap				Clap		Clap	

3	a	&	a	4	a	&	a
		Clap		Clap			

So, we're keeping the Tresillo as the first half of the rhythm, and we're adding in the second half of the rhythm, which completes the 'Clave'.

From the previous stages, I think you've worked out how to set this up, so I'm going to leave it to you to use the techniques from the first four stages.

If you're not entirely confident yet, take a look back and remind yourself of the way to work with your group. First, break it in half and get the whole group working on each half. Then stick it all together and get them to copy you. After that, turn around the speech and the clapping. With the Clave, I think it helps to imagine:

1	2	3	1	2	3	1	2	1	2	1	2	1	2	1	2
d			d			d				d		d			

Note that the 'd' always lands on '1'.

Developing the vocal parts:

In Stage 4, we developed our melody line to include three different notes on the scale. It looks like this:

1	&	2	&	3	&	4	&
Doh			Ray	Me	Ray		
C4			D4	E4	D4		

5	&	6	&	7	&	8	&
Ti			Doh				
B4			C4				

Now we're going to add in two new notes to create a different melody part.

Use this code to see how the Clave Rhythm works.

Here's the keyboard again:

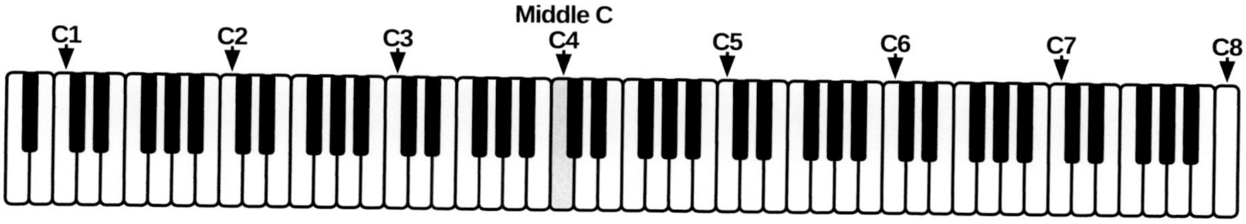

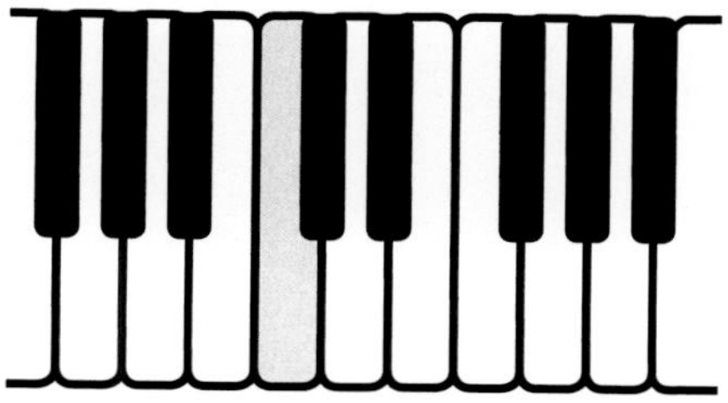

In the picture you can see G3 and A4, and you can also see G4 and A5. If you're singing with girls or boys with voices that have yet to change, you should use the higher notes (G4 and A5).

If you are working with boys with changed voices, you should use the lower notes (G3 and A4). If you have a mixture of the two, it's not a problem to have everyone singing at the pitch that works best for them.

So, those are the two notes that you're going to be using. This is how we're going to make it work rhythmically:

7	a	&	a	8	a	&	a	1	a	&	a
		So		So		La		So		So	
		G4		G4		A5		G4		G4	

You'll see here that I've opted to put in the notes for the higher pitched voices. Just change the numbers to G3 and A4 if you want to vary this. You'll also see that this rhythm starts at 7 and runs across the end of the section. This is going to give a call-and-response feel between different groups, and I would normally find this easier to demonstrate with your assistants by getting them to sing the other melody and the pop beat.

That looks like this:

ASSISTANT 1:

1	&	2	&	3	&	4	&
Dm		T	T	Ksh		T	T

5	&	6	&	7	&	8	&
Dm		T	T	Ksh		T	T

1	&	2	&	3	&	4	&
Dm		T	T	Ksh		T	T

5	&	6	&	7	&	8	&
Dm		T	T	Ksh		T	T

ASSISTANT 2: SET UP THE MELODY –

1	&	2	&	3	&	4	&
Doh			Ray		Me	Ray	
C4			D4		E4	D4	

5	&	6	&	7	&	8	&
Ti			Doh				
B4			C4				

1	&	2	&	3	&	4	&
Doh			Ray		Me	Ray	
C4			D4		E4	D4	

5	&	6	&	7	&	8	&
Ti			Doh				
B4			C4				

YOU:

1	&	2	&	3	&	4	&

5	&	6	&	7	&	8	&
					So	So	La
					G4	G4	A5

1	&	2	&	3	&	4	&
So	So						
G4	G4						

5	&	6	&	7	&	8	&
					So	So	La
					G4	G4	A5

Now let's get the group doing this with you:

YOU: Ok, (names of Assistants 1 & 2), you're going to keep the pop beat and the first melody going. Everyone else, with me. So, let's set up the rhythms... Assistants, are you ready? Ok, Assistant 1 first... after 4... 1, 2, 3, 4... (Assistant 1 starts)... Great. Now, Assistant 2, are you ready? Here we go... 1, 2, 3, 4... (Assistant 2 starts).

Assistants 1 and 2 keep this going.

YOU: Everyone else, are you ready? Here we go... (now wait for Assistant 2's melody to reach the right point and lead the whole group through the second melody passage).

Repeat this twice, or until everyone is comfortable with it.

YOU: Use instruction 4 ◉ to stop everyone.

Note: Silence, as we discussed in Stage 4, can be very tricky to deal with as a large group. This little melody segment requires the group to wait for a long time before starting. If you need to help them, count the numbers up to seven while your assistants keep their layers going. Then encourage the group to think these numbers as they prepare to come in with you.

Some people like to count numbers and develop the musical layers analytically. Others will like to feel the music and respond to the sequence which has been set up aurally around them. It's great to be aware that both these styles of learning are fine, and you should try to facilitate both.

Now that we've learned this new layer, we can finish the session by putting together the various new segments from Stage 5. You can divide the whole group into three or four parts to do this.

The four possible layers will look like this when they work together:

LAYER 1: POP BEAT

1	&	2	&	3	&	4	&
Dm		T	T	Ksh		T	T

5	&	6	&	7	&	8	&
Dm		T	T	Ksh		T	T

1	&	2	&	3	&	4	&
Dm		T	T	Ksh		T	T

5	&	6	&	7	&	8	&
Dm		T	T	Ksh		T	T

LAYER 2: MELODY 1

1	&	2	&	3	&	4	&
Doh				Ray		Me	Ray
C4				D4		E4	D4

5	&	6	&	7	&	8	&
Ti				Doh			
B4				C4			

1	&	2	&	3	&	4	&
Doh				Ray		Me	Ray
C4				D4		E4	D4

5	&	6	&	7	&	8	&
Ti				Doh			
B4				C4			

LAYER 3: CLAVE RHYTHM

1	a	&	a	2	a	&	a
Clap				Clap		Clap	

3	a	&	a	4	a	&	a
		Clap		Clap			

5	a	&	a	6	a	&	a
Clap				Clap		Clap	

7	a	&	a	8	a	&	a
		Clap		Clap			

LAYER 4: MELODY 2

1	&	2	&	3	&	4	&

5	&	6	&	7	&	8	&
					So	So	La
					G4	G4	A5

1	&	2	&	3	&	4	&
So	So						
G4	G4						

5	&	6	&	7	&	8	&
					So	So	La
					G4	G4	A5

Once you've got all of these rhythms up and running, you can start to play with the layering and dynamics. Have a look at the graphs at the start of this stage and then, with a group gaining ever increasing levels of confidence, have fun!

Notes: The Clave rhythmic pattern is used as a tool for holding the tempo together in Afro-Cuban music, such as Rumba, Salsa and Latin-Jazz. The five-stroke Clave pattern represents the structural core of many Afro-Cuban rhythms. Just as a keystone holds an arch in place, the Clave pattern holds the rhythm together in Afro-Cuban music. The Clave pattern originated in sub-Saharan African music traditions, where it serves essentially the same function as it does in Cuba. The pattern is also found in the African diaspora music of Haitian Vodou drumming, Afro-Brazilian music and Afro-Uruguayan music (Candombe). The Clave pattern is used in North American popular music as a rhythmic motif or ostinato, or simply a form of rhythmic decoration.

A pentatonic scale is a musical scale or mode with five notes per octave in contrast to heptatonic (seven note) scales such as the major scale and minor scale. Pentatonic scales are very common and are found all over the world. They are divided into those without semitones (anhemitonic) and those with (hemitonic).

According to traditional theory, the Yo scale, which does not contain semitones, is a pentatonic scale used in much Japanese music including gagaku and shomyo. The Yo scale is used specifically in folk songs and early popular songs and is contrasted with the In scale which does contain semitones. The In scale is described as 'dark' while the Yo scale is described as 'bright' sounding.

Follow this link to hear how you complete the Pentatonic Scale.

END OF STAGE 5

6 Indian rhythm, pop beat and melodic lines

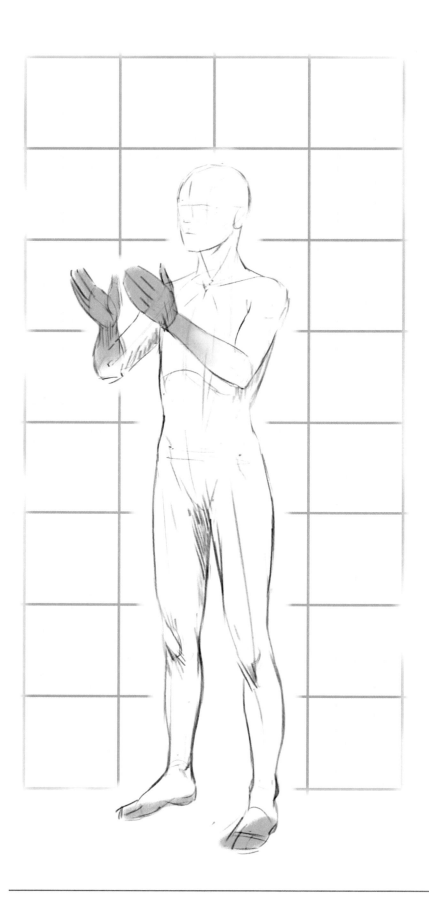

CLAP YOUR HANDS

Did you want an introduction to Stage 6? Well, you'll have to wait a while! For now, let's dive straight in:

YOU: Dha

THEM: Dha

YOU: Dhin

THEM: Dhin

YOU: Dha Dhin Dhin Dha

THEM: Dha Dhin Dhin Dha

YOU: Repeat this once.

THEM: They copy you.

YOU: Tin

THEM: Tin

YOU: Ta

THEM: Ta

YOU: Dha Tin Tin Ta

THEM: Dha Tin Tin Ta

YOU: Repeat this once.

THEM: They copy you.

YOU: Ta Dhin Dhin Dha

THEM: Ta Dhin Dhin Dha

YOU: Very good. Now this:

1	&	2	&	3	&	4	&
Dha	Dhin	Dhin	Dha	Dha	Dhin	Dhin	Dha
Clap				Clap			

THEM: They copy you.

YOU: Repeat this twice.

THEM: They copy you.

YOU: Good. Now this:

1	&	2	&	3	&	4	&
Dha	Tin	Tin	Ta	Ta	Dhin	Dhin	Dha
Wave				Clap			

THEM: They copy you.

YOU: Repeat this twice.

THEM: They copy you.

YOU: Good. Now the whole thing:

1	&	2	&	3	&	4	&
Dha	Dhin	Dhin	Dha	Dha	Dhin	Dhin	Dha
Clap				Clap			

1	&	2	&	3	&	4	&
Dha	Tin	Tin	Ta	Ta	Dhin	Dhin	Dha
Wave				Clap			

THEM: They copy you.

YOU: Repeat this twice.

THEM: They copy you.

Now we're going to add in a pitch. Here's the keyboard:

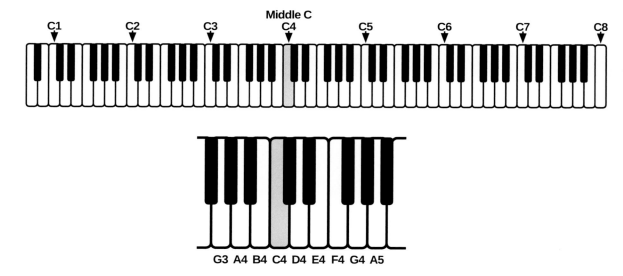

Use this code to see Paul demonstrate
the Indian rhythm, the Tintal.

1	&	2	&	3	&	4	&
Dha	Dhin	Dhin	Dha	Dha	Dhin	Dhin	Dha
E4	E4	E4	E4	F4	F4	F4	F4
Clap				Clap			

1	&	2	&	3	&	4	&
Dha	Tin	Tin	Ta	Ta	Dhin	Dhin	Dha
F4	F4	F4	F4	E4	E4	E4	E4
Wave				Clap			

You'll note that the melodic line of the first half is reversed for the second half of this section.

As with the previous stage, choose the pitch depending on the group you are working with. This has been written for higher voices but, as in the previous stage, just change any '4' to a '3' to make it work for lower voices.

And welcome to Stage 6! The great news is that, while you might have been looking for an introduction to explain what was going on, you've already done the hard bit and learned the major new element of this stage.

When you reach a level where your group is increasingly aware of how the process works, diving straight in with a good piece of new learning will be possible, and will keep them on their toes. Once the group has learned this new segment, we can start adding layers, as you're about to see.

The section you've just learned is based on the Indian 'Tintal'. Tin means 'Three' and Tal means 'Clap' in Hindi, so this literally means 'Three Claps'. You can see why the rhythm has this name from the way the actions go with the spoken and then sung syllables: three claps and one wave make up the Tintal.

And now, with your assistants, you can start to build layers, as with the previous stages.

In this stage, now that you've had a chance to play with leading all of the different sections, why not try devolving responsibility to your assistants so that they can control their sections of the group with the key instructions?

As you'll all be working together, it will be really interesting to see how each of your assistants responds to the others. When one assistant makes their group louder, will the others respond by doing the same or by making their groups quieter? Neither response would be right or wrong; the test of quality comes in the directions being given and the way that each group is responding.

The Tintal gives you a new pattern and also gives you an added harmony which will work with the previous melodies. Here's how these would fit together:

GROUP 1:

Dha	Dhin	Dhin	Dha	Dha	Dhin	Dhin	Dha
E4	E4	E4	E4	F4	F4	F4	F4
Clap				Clap			

5	&	6	&	7	&	8	&
Dha	Tin	Tin	Ta	Ta	Dhin	Dhin	Dha
F4	F4	F4	F4	E4	E4	E4	E4
Wave				Clap			

GROUP 2: WITH HAND ACTIONS... SEE NOTES IN STAGE 3, PAGE 25

1	&	2	&	3	&	4	&

5	&	6	&	7	&	8	&
					So	So	La
					G4	G4	A5

1	&	2	&	3	&	4	&
So	So						
G4	G4						

5	&	6	&	7	&	8	&
					So	So	La
					G4	G4	A5

GROUP 3: WITH HAND ACTIONS... REMEMBER NOTES IN STAGE 3, PAGE 25

1	&	2	&	3	&	4	&
Doh			Ray				
C4			D4				

5	&	6	&	7	&	8	&
Ti			Doh				
B4			C4				

GROUP 4: POP BEAT (NEW!) WITH ACTIONS

1	&	2	&	3	&	4	&
Dm	T	K	T	Ksh		T	T

5	&	6	&	7	&	8	&
Dm	T	K	T	Ksh		T	T

As these four layers start to work together, the group will enter a new sound world – which opens new doors in terms of understanding new rhythms and reaching into more complex musical challenges – without even realizing that the level of complexity has gone up.

Note on Group 2: In this little outline, you can see that there is a mention of hand movements for Group 2. Did you notice that the notes that we learned in the last stage have corresponding hand movements in the diagram at the end of Stage 3? As with the other hand movements that we have discussed, make sure that when your assistants and your groups are doing the actions, they make them as physically strong as possible, and also try to make the actions fit as precisely as possible with the relevant rhythms.

Notes on anything which you think is new: The first few stages show you how to break down all of the components of each layer. With anything new, if you want to take more time working with your group to learn these various new elements, use the same method. Break the layer into smaller chunks and work with a call and response method, first as a whole group and then, using your assistants, in smaller groups. By now, I think you're familiar with this method, so just make sure that, in the heat of the moment, these thought processes become default settings for you and your team of assistants.

Note on Group 4: You'll see that this is a modified rhythm which again adds an extra touch of complexity. We call this a syncopated rhythm. Although you change the rhythm, don't change the basic actions that go with this pattern. It's a good exercise to have the voice and body doing different things, and both voice and body hit the strong beats together, so this should still feel fairly comfortable.

Notes on the Tintal: Tintal (or Teental or Trital) is one of the most famous Talas of Hindustani music. It is also the most common Tal in North India. The structure of Tintal is so symmetrical that it presents a very simple rhythmic structure against which a performance can be laid. Note the Bols (the syllables you pronounce in the rhythm, and which correspond with a certain type of method for striking the drum with your hand) used for the first beat of each division: Dhaa, a Bol involving both hands, is played at the beginning of the first, second and final divisions; for the Khali section (third section), Naa – a right hand Bol – is used to indicate that the division is open. This 'open' Bol is the reason for the name 'Tintal' (Three Claps).

7 Layer Building

STOP

We now have a wonderful assortment of tools to play with. That's the way I like to see each of these layers that we've been learning. Imagine you have a toolbox, and each time you learn something new, you're adding a new tool to the kit.

In this section we're going to look at a structure that shows an order of adding and grouping different layers (as well as including one or two new ones) so that you can get the most out of your toolkit.

Making music can be like cooking, or making a great cocktail. There are so many ingredients to choose from, and certain ingredients work really well together.

If you put the right ingredients together in an order that works for them, you can create a masterpiece. Sometimes the same ingredients used in a different order can work well too, but sometimes things don't work so well. Here's an order to try which uses a lovely combination of all of the layers that we've learned so far.

GROUP 1: POP BEAT WITH ACTIONS

1	&	2	&	3	&	4	&
Dm	T	K	T	Ksh		T	T

5	&	6	&	7	&	8	&
Dm	T	K	T	Ksh		T	T

GROUP 2: CLAVE RHYTHM (SOUTH AMERICAN)

1	&	2	&	3	&	4	&
Clap			Clap			Clap	

5	&	6	&	7	&	8	&
		Clap		Clap			

GROUP 3: STANDARD PATTERN (AFRICAN)

1	2	3	4	5	6	7	8	9	10	11	12	13	14	15	16
Cha			Cha			Cha	Cha			Cha		Cha			Cha

Stop Group 2 and Group 3. Now add in:

GROUP 4: MELODIC LINE 1

1	&	2	&	3	&	4	&
Doh				Ray			
C4				D4			

5	&	6	&	7	&	8	&
Ti				Doh			
B4				C4			

GROUP 5: TINTAL (INDIAN)

Dha	Dhin	Dhin	Dha	Dha	Dhin	Dhin	Dha
E4	E4	E4	E4	F4	F4	F4	F4
Clap			Clap				

5	&	6	&	7	&	8	&
Dha	Tin	Tin	Ta	Ta	Dhin	Dhin	Dha
F4	F4	F4	F4	E4	E4	E4	E4

GROUP 6: MELODIC LINE 2

1	&	2	&	3	&	4	&

5	&	6	&	7	&	8	&
					So	So	La
					G4	G4	A5

1	&	2	&	3	&	4	&
So	So						
G4	G4						

5	&	6	&	7	&	8	&
					So	So	La
					G4	G4	A5

Stop Group 1.

Now add in Group 2, followed by Group 3.

Bring the volume of all groups down.

Stop Group 4 and Group 5.

Bring the volume of Group 2, 3 and 6 up.

Now add in Group 1.

Add in Group 4 and Group 5. Start these two groups quietly.

Bring up the volume of all groups.

Let the groups continue around twice more and then stop Group 6.

Now stop Group 4 and 5.

You are left with Groups 1, 2 and 3. Let them carry on twice more and then stop them all at the same time.

End of Piece.

Two new ideas:

Here's another rhythm for you to put into your toolkit. This is a rhythm heavily associated with a Reggae beat:

1	a	&	a	2	a	&	a
		Ja	Da			Ja	Da

3	a	&	a	4	a	&	a
		Ja	Da			Ja	Da

Put this with the Pop Beat to see how this feels:

1	a	&	a	2	a	&	a
Dm				T		T	
Clap			Clap			Clap	

3	a	&	a	4	a	&	a
Ksh				T		T	
Clap			Clap			Clap	

With the Pop beat, you can see that the Tresillo beat is underneath it. Try to fit these three together; varying the speed of all of these rhythms is great fun. Start slowly, but really practice getting a good fast tempo going. When you achieve a faster speed, all of these rhythms will begin to sound amazing when they link together.

With this Reggae feel, try to put a bit of an accent on the 'J' of 'Ja'. That will help you and everyone taking part feel where this part of the offbeat is. We call this 'offbeat' because the rhythm happens between the numbers rather than on the numbers. The opposite of 'offbeat' is 'onbeat'. The very first Pop beat that we learned in Stage 1 is a good example of an 'onbeat' rhythm.

Use this code to see how the Reggae rhythm works.

A new melody line (Melody 1B):

1	a	2	&	3	&	4	&
Doh				Ti			
C4				B4			

5	a	6	&	7	&	8	&
So				So			
G3				G3			

We are going to fit this to the same rhythm as the first melody line, and start it on the same note. To save you flicking back, here's the keyboard again:

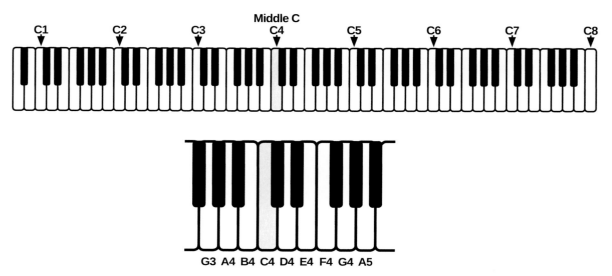

G3 A4 B4 C4 D4 E4 F4 G4 A5

As before, if these notes (written for the lower voices) are too low, you can put them up so that C4 becomes C5, B4 becomes B5 and G3 becomes G4.

Adding this line to the 'Melody 1' line will actually start to create a harmonic feel, and you, with your assistants and the groups, should find these quite easy to put together.

To build these two together, start with Melody 1B and then add in Melody 1 (which everyone will know well by now).

EVERYONE: MELODY 1

1	&	2	&	3	&	4	&
Doh				Ray			
C4				D4			

5	a	6	&	7	&	8	&
Ti				Doh			
B4				C4			

Your assistants continue while you sing this – then the whole group copies you:

YOU AND THE WHOLE GROUP: MELODY 1B

1	&	2	&	3	&	4	&
Doh				Ti			
C4				B4			

5	a	6	&	7	&	8	&
So				So			
G3				G3			

Once you've done this, split the group into two, with one group doing each of the melodies. Once this has been set up successfully, swap the groups over, so that by the time you stop, both groups have done both melodies.

Now, if you're feeling adventurous, try splitting the group into four, putting these four layers together:

GROUP 1: POP BEAT WITH ACTIONS

1	&	2	&	3	&	4	&
Dm	T	K	T	Ksh		T	T

5	&	6	&	7	&	8	&
Dm	T	K	T	Ksh		T	T

GROUP 2: MELODY 1

1	&	2	&	3	&	4	&
Doh				Ray			
C4				D4			

5	&	6	&	7	&	8	&
Ti				Doh			
B4				C4			

GROUP 3: MELODY 1B

1	&	2	&	3	&	4	&
Doh				Ti			
C4				B4			

5	&	6	&	7	&	8	&
So				So			
G3				G3			

GROUP 4: TINTAL RHYTHM (INDIAN)

1	&	2	&	3	&	4	&
Dha	Dhin	Dhin	Dha	Dha	Dhin	Dhin	Dha
E4	E4	E4	E4	F4	F4	F4	F4
Wave				Clap			

5	&	6	&	7	&	8	&
Dha	Tin	Tin	Ta	Ta	Dhin	Dhin	Dha
F4	F4	F4	F4	E4	E4	E4	E4
Clap				Clap			

With the Group 4 rhythm, accent the 'Dha' and 'Ta' syllables a little. This will help to create some great rhythms and accent the harmony shifts.

Do follow the order of building the groups up as laid out here, as this will make the most sense to the groups as they take part.

By the time you've had practice developing the ideas of structure, while implementing these new rhythms and melodies, you'll be getting a great feel for some complicated rhythms and harmonies.

It is important to stress that most of these different layers have either hand actions to fit with the rhythms or elements of physical percussion (clap, click and thigh slap are the key ones). This is an important part of the mental process that this Method develop – and also creates a great displacement device for the vocal work. I would encourage you to start the process of learning each layer with physical activity, as outlined all the way back in Stage 1.

Notes on Reggae: Reggae is most easily recognized by the rhythmic accents on the offbeat (or back beat), usually played by guitar or piano (or both), known as the skank. This pattern accents the second and fourth beat in each bar (or the 'and's of each beat depending on how the music is counted) and combines with the drum emphasis on beat three to create a unique feel and sense of phrasing in contrast to most other popular genres' focus on beat one, the "downbeat". The tempo of reggae is usually felt as slower than the popular Jamaican forms, ska and rocksteady, which preceded it. It is this slower tempo, the guitar/piano offbeats, the emphasis on the third beat, and the use of syncopated, melodic bass lines that differentiates reggae from other music, although other musical styles have incorporated some of these innovations separately.

8 Conclusions
a few new ideas
and future
developments

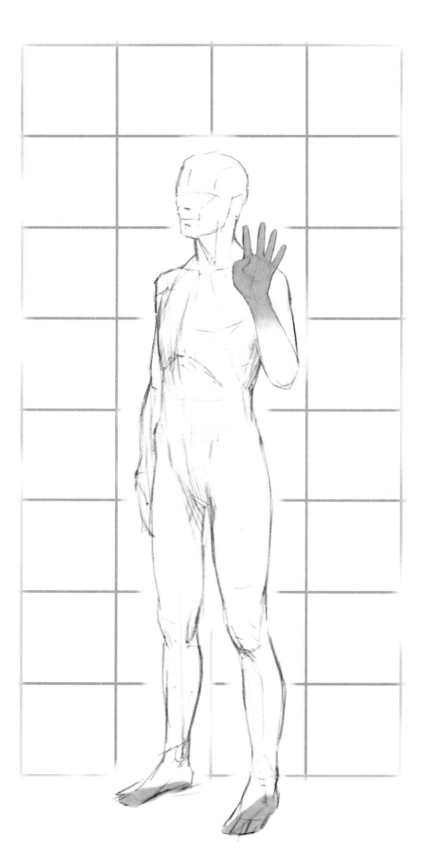

AFTER FOUR

Congratulations! You've made it to the last stage and, in the process, have covered a course that will introduce your group to a variety of rhythms and musical ideas from around the world.

Every rhythm, syllable, action and melodic motif in this first book of the VOCES8 Method has been chosen to tap into the conscious and sub-conscious learning ability of the group that you are working with. Each stage provides tools that can be learned by anyone, regardless of previous musical experience. The Method gives you all you need to know to lead a simple series of sessions that grow in complexity, but in a step-by-step progression, which means that each and every new element can be learned with ease.

Importantly, this Method also encourages you to train a team of your students to take on leadership roles in these eight-minute sessions. This isn't necessary for you to be able to run the VOCES8 Method, but I would encourage you to pursue this opportunity. The students will gain immensely from being given the chance to lead groups, and you'll also find that there will be those who are keen to assist you who might not be perceived as the leading musicians in your school or group. You can encourage those who want to be involved to practise and achieve the role of assistant but make sure those who are taking on these roles are excited by the challenge and keen to work sufficiently hard to be successful.

The purpose of this method is to encourage learning, and to use the brain and body in ways that activate learners. This method is unique in the sense that it has been prepared from a musical background, but created so as to be able to be led by anyone, and so that everyone taking part in this process will be better prepared for learning after they have taken part.

While in the future, the ideas in this Method will be a launch pad for us to explore a whole world of music, be sure to start off at Stage 1 and work through this book until you reach the end. The Method has been structurally prepared to be used this way.

As you've made it this far, here's one final set of challenges to leave you with. The next stage in music-making, after we've learned to create complex rhythms and melodic blocks, is to start developing our harmonic language as well. This final passage of the VOCES8 Method takes some of the existing ideas and amends them slightly to give you a harmonic language that encompasses a considerable number of chords that we've touched on without any lengthy discussion. Instead of having one pattern, this final section gives you three patterns that can be put side by side to create a chord structure that you might hear in a pop song or two...

Enjoy, and thanks for everything you've done to open up the minds of the group you are leading.

PATTERN 1:

GROUP 1:

1	&	2	&	3	&	4	&
Dm	T	K	T	Ksh		T	T

5	&	6	&	7	&	8	&
Dm	T	K	T	Ksh		T	T

GROUP 2:

1	&	2	&	3	&	4	&
Dha	Dhin	Dhin	Dha	Dha	Dhin	Dhin	Dha
C4	C4	C4	C4	C4	C4	C4	C4
Clap				Clap			

5	&	6	&	7	&	8	&
Dha	Tin	Tin	Ta	Ta	Dhin	Dhin	Dha
C4	C4	C4	C4	C4	C4	C4	C4
Wave				Clap			

GROUP 3:

1	&	2	&	3	&	4	&
Dha	Dhin	Dhin	Dha	Dha	Dhin	Dhin	Dha
E4	E4	E4	E4	F4	F4	F4	F4
Clap				Clap			

5	&	6	&	7	&	8	&
Dha	Tin	Tin	Ta	Ta	Dhin	Dhin	Dha
F4	F4	F4	F4	E4	E4	E4	E4
Wave				Clap			

GROUP 4:

1	&	2	&	3	&	4	&
Dha	Dhin	Dhin	Dha	Dha	Dhin	Dhin	Dha
G4	G4	G4	G4	A5	A5	A5	A5
Clap				Clap			

5	&	6	&	7	&	8	&
Dha	Tin	Tin	Ta	Ta	Dhin	Dhin	Dha
A5	A5	A5	A5	G4	G4	G4	G4
Wave				Clap			

Loop this pattern a few times. You'll see that the differences come in the notes being sung by Groups 2 and 4. Group 2 is giving us a 'Pedal' note and Group 4 is giving us added harmony. The part being sung by Group 4 can be sung lower at G3 and A4 if you want.

PATTERN 2:

GROUP 1:

1	&	2	&	3	&	4	&
Dm	T	K	T	Ksh		T	T

5	&	6	&	7	&	8	&
Dm	T	K	T	Ksh		T	T

GROUP 2:

1	&	2	&	3	&	4	&
Doh			Ray				
C4			D4				

5	&	6	&	7	&	8	&
Ti			Doh				
B4			C4				

GROUP 3:

1	&	2	&	3	&	4	&
Doh			Ti				
C4			B4				

5	&	6	&	7	&	8	&
So			La				
G4			A4				

GROUP 4:

1	&	2	&	3	&	4	&
Dha	Dhin	Dhin	Dha	Dha	Dhin	Dhin	Dha
E4	E4	E4	E4	E4	E4	E4	E4
Clap				Clap			

5	&	6	&	7	&	8	&
Dha	Tin	Tin	Ta	Ta	Dhin	Dhin	Dha
E4	E4	E4	E4	E4	E4	E4	E4
Wave				Clap			

GROUP 5:

1	&	2	&	3	&	4	&
Dha	Dhin	Dhin	Dha	Dha	Dhin	Dhin	Dha
G4	G4	G4	G4	A5	A5	A5	A5
Clap				Clap			

5	&	6	&	7	&	8	&
Dha	Tin	Tin	Ta	Ta	Dhin	Dhin	Dha
A5	A5	A5	A5	G4	G4	G4	G4
Wave				Clap			

In this section Pattern 2, you can see that the main difference to Pattern 1 is that the 'Pedal' has been replaced by our Melodies 1 and 1b from previous stages. However, you can see that Melody 1b has a slight difference: the last note is changed. This creates a chord that ends Pattern 2, but will feel, when you hear it, unfinished. For that reason, Pattern 2 should go into Pattern 3, which finishes off the progression. You should also see that the 'Pedal' idea has moved to Groups 4 and 5. While the rhythm and action stay the same, the notes have changed so that the whole rhythm now happens on one note. This will happen again in Pattern 3.

PATTERN 3:

GROUP 1:

1	&	2	&	3	&	4	&
Dm	T	K	T	Ksh		T	T

5	&	6	&	7	&	8	&
Dm	T	K	T	Ksh		T	T

GROUP 2:

1	&	2	&	3	&	4	&
Doh				Ray			
C4				D4			

5	&	6	&	7	&	8	&
Ti				Doh			
B4				C4			

GROUP 3:

1	&	2	&	3	&	4	&
Doh				Ti			
C4				B4			

5	&	6	&	7	&	8	&
So				So			
G3				G3			

GROUP 4:

1	&	2	&	3	&	4	&
Dha	Dhin	Dhin	Dha	Dha	Dhin	Dhin	Dha
E4	E4	E4	E4	E4	E4	E4	E4
Clap				Clap			

5	&	6	&	7	&	8	&
Dha	Tin	Tin	Ta	Ta	Dhin	Dhin	Dha
E4	E4	E4	E4	E4	E4	E4	E4
Wave				Clap			

GROUP 5:

1	&	2	&	3	&	4	&
Dha	Dhin	Dhin	Dha	Dha	Dhin	Dhin	Dha
G4	G4	G4	G4	G4	G4	G4	G4
Clap				Clap			

5	&	6	&	7	&	8	&
Dha	Tin	Tin	Ta	Ta	Dhin	Dhin	Dha
G4	G4	G4	G4	G4	G4	G4	G4
Wave				Clap			

You can see here that the change is to the final note of Group 3 and creates a chord that feels like the end of our piece. In Pattern 3, Groups 4 and 5 give us our 'Pedal' feel again, while the chords in the other parts shift around them.

Once you've got these three patterns learned, you can put them together like this to create a flowing harmonic structure:

Pattern 1 – Repeat this 2 times in total

Pattern 2 – Once through

Pattern 3 – Once through

Pattern 2 – Once through

Pattern 3 – Once through

FINISH.

This gives you a structure which works harmonically. You can use all of the other rhythmic patterns in the previous stages to add layers to this structure, but you've now created a harmonic structure which will open the door to all sorts of music in the future.

Conclusion: The end of the beginning.

Remember that, while playing with increasingly complex harmonic language will be fun, the focus of this VOCES8 Method is on creating a series of layers that can be used in an eight-minute setting in a large group environment. The purpose of this sequence of stages is to prepare the mind and body for learning. The research on which this Method is based shows that it is these types of musical sequences that have the best transfer for the purposes of academic development.

I hope you've enjoyed working through the eight stages of the VOCES8 Method with your group. I believe that the best learning happens when we have fun, and the bonus of this programme is that there will be plenty of musical learning as a by-product of the involvement of everyone in this activity.

This Method has the capacity to unite your group, however large and regardless of the age and gender, with a series of musical games that will bring a sense of teamwork, fulfillment, achievement and expression. Following these steps will ensure that you, as the leader, are able to gain confidence in front of the group, and it will also allow you to offer your team of assistants a valuable development opportunity.

I've written this because I believe passionately in the power of music. I believe that music can make a difference to all of our lives and that this Method is a great first step for everyone. Music has a power to connect people and to enrich our lives in a way that very little else can. It is a truly life-enhancing means of communication which transcends all spoken language.

Those who show real passion and interest in this weekly eight-minute session will have their minds opened to music from across the world, and you will have shown them a gateway through which any of the group can begin to increase their knowledge in a host of different musical areas. You can do all of this without the need for expensive equipment, and you can create all sorts of wonderful pieces of music that will challenge the group you work with.

Good luck, and thank you.

Paul Smith

This code will take you to see Melody two and a final thought from Paul.

Appendix

If you thought that was it, and you're longing for a little more harmony, here's a little bit extra for you. It doesn't fit with the programme plan, in that I don't see this as an essential part of the Method, but it's a nice optional extra for anyone who wants to have a go at something with a little more harmony. We're still working from the keyboard, and I'm still keeping the range pretty close for you. This is called 'One more time'.

One More Time

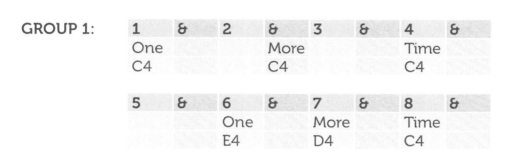

GROUP 1:

1	&	2	&	3	&	4	&
One				More		Time	
C4				C4		C4	

5	&	6	&	7	&	8	&
		One		More		Time	
		E4		D4		C4	

Do this twice, then add in:

GROUP 2:

1	&	2	&	3	&	4	&
One				More		Time	
C4				B4		A4	

5	&	6	&	7	&	8	&
		One		More		Time	
		G3		G3		G3	

Do this twice, then add in:

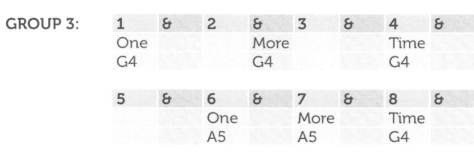

GROUP 3:

1	&	2	&	3	&	4	&
One				More		Time	
G4				G4		G4	

5	&	6	&	7	&	8	&
		One		More		Time	
		A5		A5		G4	

Do this twice, then add in:

GROUP 4:

1	&	2	&	3	&	4	&
Da				Da	Na		Da
F3				F3	F3		G3

5	&	6	&	7	&	8	&
		Da	Na		Da	Na	
		G3	G3		G3	G3	

Now stop Group 2 and give them this new part:

GROUP 2 (b):

1	&	2	&	3	&	4	&
Da				Da	Na		Da
A4				A4	A4		B4

5	&	6	&	7	&	8	&
		Da	Na		Da	Na	
		B4	B4		B4	B4	

Now stop Group 3 and give them this new part:

GROUP 3 (b):

1	&	2	&	3	&	4	&
Da	Na	Na		Da	Na	Na	
G4	G4	G4		A5	A5	A5	

5	&	6	&	7	&	8	&
Da	Na		Da	Na		Da	Na
G4	G4		A5	A5		G4	G4

Now stop Group 1 and give them this new part:

GROUP 1 (b):

1	&	2	&	3	&	4	&
Da	Na					Da	Na
C4	C4					C4	C4

5	&	6	&	7	&	8	&
Da	Na	Na		Da	Na	Na	
C4	C4	C4		C4	C4	C4	

Now stop Group 2 and Group 4. Move Group 2 back to the first part:

GROUP 2:

1	&	2	&	3	&	4	&
One				More		Time	
C4				B4		A4	

5	&	6	&	7	&	8	&
		One		More		Time	
		G3		G3		G3	

Now put all groups back onto their first parts:

GROUP 1:

1	&	2	&	3	&	4	&
One				More		Time	
C4				C4		C4	

5	&	6	&	7	&	8	&
		One		More		Time	
		E4		D4		C4	

GROUP 3:

1	&	2	&	3	&	4	&
One				More		Time	
G4				G4		G4	

5	&	6	&	7	&	8	&
		One		More		Time	
		A5		A5		G4	

GROUP 4:

1	&	2	&	3	&	4	&
Da				Da	Na	Da	
F3				F3	F3	G3	

5	&	6	&	7	&	8	&
		Da	Na		Da	Na	
		G3	G3		G3	G3	

Finally, change Group 4 onto this part:

GROUP 4 (b):

1	&	2	&	3	&	4	&
One				More		Time	
F3				F3		G3	

5	&	6	&	7	&	8	&
		One		More		Time	
		G3		G3		F3	

And to finish, make each group stop in the following place and hold that last note until you bring all groups off:

GROUP 1:

1	&	2	&	3	&	4	&
One				More		Time	
C4				C4		C4	

5	&	6	&	7	&	8	&
		One		More		Time	
		E4		D4		E4	

GROUP 2:

1	&	2	&	3	&	4	&
One				More		Time	
C4				B4		A4	

5	&	6	&	7	&	8	&
		One		More		Time	
		G3		G3		C4	

GROUP 3:

1	&	2	&	3	&	4	&
One				More		Time	
G4				G4		G4	

5	&	6	&	7	&	8	&
		One		More		Time	
		A5		A5		G4	

GROUP 4:

1	&	2	&	3	&	4	&
One				More		Time	
F3				F3		G3	

5	&	6	&	7	&	8	&
		One		More		Time	
		G3		G3		F3	

Then... 1, 2, 3, 4... stop!

Note: You can have a Pop beat running all the way through this if you want... Or any of the other beats for that matter.

Other notes:

1. During all of these stages, play around with the tempo that you're using. I'd suggest you try to get to a tempo of around 120 beats per minute, which means that there should be two beats per second. In time, you should be able to go faster, but this is a good place to start.

2. Try varying between long notes and short notes. In passages which have notes and spaces, see what happens when you try long joined-up notes and short spiky notes. It can create two very different effects.

END OF APPENDIX

References

Books:

Peñalosa, David. (2009). The Clave Matrix; Afro-Cuban Rhythm: Its Principles and African Origins, page 21. Redway, CA: Bembe Inc. ISBN 1-886502-80-3

Jones, A.M. (1959). Studies in African Music. page 210–213. OUP 1978 edition: ISBN 0-19-713512-9.

Landis, Beth. (1972). The Eclectic Curriculum in American Music Education: Contributions of Dalcroze, Kodaly, and Orff. Music Educators National Conference 1972, ISBN-10: 0940796031

Benward, Bruce & Saker, Marilyn (2003). Music: In Theory and Practice, Vol. I, p.37. Mcgraw-Hill College, Seventh Edition. ISBN 978-0-07-294262-0.

Titon, Jeff Todd (1996). Worlds of Music: An Introduction to the Music of the World's Peoples, p.372. Cengage Learning; 3 edition (January 5, 2009) ISBN 0-02-872612-X.

Roberts, John Storm (1979). The Latin tinge: the impact of Latin American music on the United States. Oxford University Press, USA; 2 edition (January 21, 1999) ISBN-10: 0195121015

Levitin, Daniel J. (2006). This Is Your Brain On Music, pp. 113–114 Plume/Penguin; 1 Reprint edition (August 28, 2007) ISBN 978-0-452-28852-2.

Articles:

Hallam, S. (2010) 'The power of music: its impact of the intellectual, personal and social development of children and young people', p269–289. International Journal of Music Education 38(3), SAGE Publications Ltd

Kubik, Gerhard cited by Agawu, Kofi (2006: 1–46). "Structural Analysis or Cultural Analysis? Comparing Perspectives on the 'Standard Pattern' of West African Rhythm" Journal of the American Musicological Society v. 59, n. 1 p.1–46. University of California Press

Websites:

University of Wisconsin-Green Bay. "Japanese Music" in Cross-Cultural Communication: World Music. University of Wisconsin-Green Bay. http://web.archive.org/web/20080313144427/http://www.uwgb.edu/ogradyt/world/japan.htm (accessed July 26, 2013)

All About Jazz (2009). "Various Artists | Rocksteady: The Roots Of Reggae". http://www.allaboutjazz.com/php/article.php?id=34239#.UfOlVZh5nzI (accessed July 26, 2013)